Be F.R.E.E.

Tiffanie Y. Lewis

Be F.R.E.E.
Tiffanie Y. Lewis

Published by Lewisland Press
Lewislandpress@gmail.com

Copyright © 2024 by Tiffanie Y. Lewis
All rights reserved. No part of this book may be reproduced in any form or by any electronic or mechanical means, including information storage and retrieval or mechanical means without permission in writing from the publisher, except by a reviewer who may quote brief passages in a review.

ISBN: 979-8-218-51182-1 Paperback

Dedicated to you

May you find a way to embrace yourself wholly.

May you rediscover how truly wonderful you are.

May you love and accept every part of yourself, and do not worry about who does not.

May you be present with who you are right now, and release yourself from the burden of who you are not.

May you be free to always be you.

That is my intention for you, and for women around the world.

TABLE OF CONTENTS

Be	7
Forget the Past	14
Remember Who You Are	24
Emerge From Failures and Worry	32
Embrace Your Future	44

BE

*"To be or not to be
That is the question…"*

Shakespeare wrote one of the most popular soliloquies in history. This challenging question can be interpreted in so many ways. This small word, "be", can be so empowering. Alone it has many meanings. Yet, when conjugated with other verbs it can express even more powerful declarations. I don't want to get into a grammar lesson here, so I'll illustrate my point with a few examples.

The verb "to be" can have past, present and future contexts. The past can represent characteristics of a person, place or a thing. For example, "I was upset." That is a past description of how a person felt at one point in time. In the present, "to be" means "to exist". "I am alive," for instance. In the future, "to be" gives an expectation of what will occur. "I will be fine tomorrow." Now, with that brief, and simple explanation, let me make my point.

In this book, I hope to encourage you to acknowledge your past. It's okay to consider your experiences, feelings and thoughts from yesterday, or even years ago. However, limit that consideration so that today does not become consumed by yesterday. Today is a precious gift. So be present in it. Exist. Live!

Ask yourself, what can I do for myself

today to make it a better day? It's important to ask yourself this question because no one else in the world knows the answer to it. Sure, someone can give you flowers, buy you a meal or send you a funny video that might brighten your day. But they are guessing at what would bring you joy today. Only you know what would truly elevate your experience today. So what is that?

I remember reaching a point in my life when I had accomplished everything on my goals list. I don't mean my goals for the year, I mean my BHAGs - my big, hairy audacious goals! I had the job I was hoping for. I owned the home I was saving for. I had the car I wanted to drive. I had published my first book. I was speaking all over the country. I'd achieved my savings goals. I was growing spiritually. I felt like I had run out of dreams and, for months, I couldn't envision what was next for me. Before I knew it, I was depressed. I found myself comparing my life to others around me and even though I'd accomplished a lot, I felt like I hadn't done enough.

I wish I could remember exactly what snapped me out of it. Nevertheless, I know it was a combination of things like a trip to another country, a conversation with my confidants and something I read that inspired me. In all of that, I discovered that in order for me to live, I needed to focus on being me.

While it's okay to draw inspiration from others' accomplishments or lifestyles, it's not okay to belittle yourself for not achieving or acquiring what they have. You don't have to be someone you're not to be amazing. You're already amazing! Be the amazing you! Discover who you are by exploring things life has to offer you.

While we were growing up, my parents took my siblings and I all over the country. We even went to Canada and Mexico before I was in high school. (To this day my siblings and I can remember a man with an oversized foot selling sunglasses in Tijuana!) I developed a love for travel and now, my name is synonymous with travel to everyone who knows me. My own father calls me and says, "What country are you in?", and nobody ever believes me when I say, "I'm home."

Tiffanie Y. Lewis

I'm sharing this to say that I learned something new about myself as I explored the world. Each city and country I've visited taught me more about God, people and myself. Travel became my way of getting to know me and discovering who I am. What's your way of discovering you? Is it art? Reading? Skating? Fishing? Higher education? Snowmobiling? Playing games? Puzzles? Exercise? Going to museums, Broadway shows or art galleries? Whatever your hobbies are, they are good ways to learn more about yourself. Make time for them. Make "you" a priority. Why? Because there's only one "you."

So just be. Live! This is where we conjugate (add words to) the verb "be" to give us those powerful declarations. Here is

Be F.R.E.E.

what I like to call the ABC's of being or the "Be Manifesto":

Be Amazing. **Be Bold.** Be Curious.
Be **Daring.** Be Enthusiastic.
BE FREE
Be **Grateful.** Be Humble.
BE IMPACTFUL. **Be Joyful.**
Be Kind. Be Loving. Be Malleable. Be Nice.
BE OPTIMISTIC.
BE PROUD. Be Quotable.
Be Reliable. Be Sincere. Be Thoughtful.
BE UNIQUE. Be Versatile. Be Witty.
Be Xenial. Be Youthful.
BE ZESTFUL.

FORGET THE PAST

*N*ow, hear me out. I'm not saying don't reflect on your history. Rather, I am admonishing you not to dwell in any part of your past that brings on a slew of negative emotions. Don't dwell on any of these things:

- who did it
- why they did it
- where they did it
- with whom they did it it
- who saw them when they did it
- who saw them do it
- who didn't see them do it, but talks about it anyway

Be F.R.E.E.

- who remembers it and brings it up all the time
- where you were when you heard it
- what song you were listening to
- what day of the week it was
- what month it was
- what year it was

Forget about it! Let it go! How? Consider this… Some of us, especially women, hold on to past events, actions or mistreatment we've experienced from others with such a tight grip that we miss embracing the reality of what is happening today. We can be so stuck on how badly we were treated by a man that we blame every man we meet for the wrong doings of the first guy. As a result, we miss an opportunity to love and to be loved because we are stuck with the memory of those who didn't love us right. The same is true for our relationship with our friends or family.

Unfortunately, even blood doesn't keep people from hurting us. I don't know about you but I grew up thinking that family had to stick together no matter what. But then I realized I was trying to stick with some family members who weren't sticking with me. Rather than remain angry, confused, bitter or become vengeful, I sought ways to release them and, in some cases, when I paused and reflected, I realized they had released me and I was the one (as they say in church) yet holding on!

Another thing I've observed is that some people create toxicity by rehashing the past. They don't want to forget a negative experience and they don't want you to forget it either. In fact, some people are so toxic that they want you to remember things the way they remember it. They won't even let you have your own memories. They spend countless hours trying to get you to remember their versions of what happened and how it happened. Then, they have the audacity to get angry when you don't remember it that way or even at all.

When I was growing up, people would say, "They need Jesus!" Well, I believe that, but I also believe they need therapy! Somebody must help them with their imprisonment in the past and you don't have to be that person. I have a degree in Clinical/Community psychology so I've learned a thing or two about abnormal human behavior. I've recently found myself saying, "I'm sorry, I don't have the degree for that." I'm telling you, some of these things that people do require someone with more degrees than I have! But I know enough to know when enough is enough and, if I want to live, I need to choose a separate path and go on with my life.

Forgetting can be a healthy coping mechanism. It relieves you from the stress associated with remembering a difficult moment and the feelings associated with it. My therapist enlightened me to the fact that the body doesn't forget. Emotions come from your mind, body or spirit remembering a feeling that occurred at one time or another. Don't believe me? Think about the best kiss you've ever had. See what I mean? Did you close your eyes? Do you remember that feeling? Do you remember his name? Mmhmm, that's why I just said kiss; I don't want you to stop reading and make a phone call.

Alright, get it together. Come back with me. Now, since your body remembers and can evoke feelings you've felt previously, you have to be careful what you rehash with your mind and with your mouth. Letting things go means:

1. Acknowledge that what was, was…and declare that it is no more
2. If it is still true, consider the options to change your circumstances
3. When you change, give yourself permission to move on

One of the ways I needed to move on

from pain and toxicity was seeking counseling. I sought it from multiple sources. My mother, my favorite aunt, my grandparents, my colleagues, my pastor, and my mentors all provide some value at different points in time. There is safety in hearing wisdom from sage voices. Some of those voices were new and some I've had my entire life. However, all opinions were not good for me and I had to filter out which ones didn't work for me.

I had reached a point when I needed something consistent and disciplined to help me sort out my thoughts and feelings. I needed to do this with someone who was constructive and would give me practical steps that could produce long-term, positive results. My friend referred me to a therapist who I now meet with weekly (unless I'm crazy busy). I make every effort to keep my weekly appointment because that is the time that I'm investing in my mental health and wellbeing.

It's my time and no one can do that for me. I must follow through on my commitment to myself. If you can't commit to yourself, good luck with fully committing to anything or anyone else. I decided that I must show up for myself to be a better version of myself. It also keeps me from trying to duplicate someone else or worse, trying to be a person that someone else wants me to be.

Beloved, do yourself a favor and do not dwell in the past. Live in the present. It is the only thing that's promised. Tomorrow we might not be so lucky, so we must make the most of today. Be present. Be good to yourself. Be kind to yourself. My life is not over and yours isn't either. I'm still working on me, but I declare while I'm working on me, I'm going to be free!

Questions for Consideration

1. What do you need to accept and acknowledge?
2. What can you declare from this point forward?
3. What can you change?
4. What type of support do you need to move on?
5. How can you be more kind to yourself?

Be F.R.E.E.

Affirmation: I cannot change the past. I do not need to change the past. I only need to live for today.

REMEMBER WHO YOU ARE

One of the most fundamental, existential questions we have to answer for ourselves is "who am I?" The answer seems to elude us as we continue to search for our purpose in life. I've found that the answer is much simpler than we think. Sure, anything simple can be made more complex, but sometimes we really overcomplicate things and we find ourselves disappointed, stagnate and lost. Listen, just go with me on some facts and then I'll push you to exercise your faith in yourself. Deal? Okay.

Your mother and father each had to contribute something to get you here. Whether they did it by force, by love or by modern medicine, you began forming in a woman's womb and some months later, you popped out. Before you physically arrived though, your eye color, hair color, skin color, and even the number of hairs on your head were already determined in your DNA. The code that makes you uniquely you and was written before you even breathed one breath.

Your qualities and proclivities are part of what makes you unique. By the time you were five years old, your personality was already in development. Food you liked or disliked was already well known by whoever raised you. Your passions for music, art, math, science, fashion, animals, reading, or laughter were already evident to those who influenced you as a child. Can you imagine how many things had to fit perfectly into place to get you to where you are today? You are not an accident. You are a legit, certified, one-of-a-kind creation!

Here's where your faith needs to kick in. Can you believe that you were created uniquely on purpose for a purpose? Can you believe that God orchestrated the right people to be in a certain place at a certain time so you could exist right now? Before you breathed one breath, God planned for you to live. And, once He decided you would exist, there was no turning back. The record reflects that you are here! So, accept that and believe that you are His creation, His child, and He wants the best for your life.

Be F.R.E.E.

Each of us must have something to offer the world or our existence would not be necessary. Something needs you to be here. Someone needs you. Someone needs to be loved by you. Someone needs your touch, your kiss and your embrace. Someone needs to know that you care. Who is that? Who have you already done it for? Who has yet to receive your love, time and attention? That's for you to explore and to do so with intention.

Something needs to be created by you. How do I know? We were created by a Creator who made all things in His image. What is it that you should create? That's for you to explore. Just remember that your existence was intentional. So as long as you have breath in your body, you can live life with intention.

You have to determine what are the little things that make you happy, and do them. A lot of little things will add up to big things. Then, the big things add up to some real joyful moments. When I reflect on what makes me "me", I realize the core of who I am hasn't changed. I was born this way and I've learned to love me. It is a learning process because the world has so many things working to bring you down and destroy your confidence or love for yourself.

You will always be too much or too little of something to someone. A famous poet, named John Lydgate, once said, "You can please some of the people all of the time, you can please all of the people some of the time, but you can't please all of the people all of the time." The one person you have control of pleasing is yourself. So figure out what pleases you and work on that.

This is critical because if you don't work on that, you'll wake up one day, unhappy and unsure of why you're not pleased with yourself. It is not your responsibility to live up to everyone else's expectations of you. In fact, it's impossible. There are an infinite number of opinions about what you should do, when you should do it and with whom you should do it and you cannot satisfy all of those opinions.

One night after writing and looking at some notes I'd written in the past, I looked toward heaven and said, "I love everything about me!" If she had heard me, my sister would say, "Girl, you're crazy!" and we'd laugh. Nonetheless, I believe in showing myself love. I absolutely believe that being grateful for my quirks as much as my talents makes me appreciate life even more.

If you don't remember anything else I write, remember this: You deserve to be loved by you. Full stop. No ifs, ands or buts. You can't tell anybody how to love you if you don't know how to love you. You should tell the world by the way you live, "Do you want to know how to love me? Watch the ways I love me!"

𝓑𝑒 F.R.E.E.

Questions for Consideration

1. What are some things that you enjoy?
2. What are some characteristics that you love about yourself?
3. How do you show love when people need it most?
4. What have you created or what are you creating to give to the world?
5. What are some small things that delight you and allow you to show love to yourself?

Affirmation: I was born on purpose with purpose. I am unique and I deserve to be loved by me.

EMERGE FROM FAILURES AND WORRY

What is it about life that makes us strive for perfection to the point that we fear failure? Some of us are so desperately afraid of making a mistake that we lie to appear right. For whom? For what? And it's not just about being wrong, but it's as if we have programmed into society that succeeding means getting it right every time or achieving a goal on the first try.

I remember being taught a song when I was a child. "If at first you don't succeed, try and try again." But as an adult, I watch the same people that taught me that song, beat themselves up for not being perfect.

Be F.R.E.E.

It's heartbreaking.

I watched the 2024 Olympics along with millions of people around the world. I like gymnastics, swimming, volleyball, and basketball, but I have to say that track and field is my favorite competition to watch. Noah Lyles had won the 100-meter dash and was set to race the 200-meter final race just days later. Unfortunately, by the time he was supposed to race, he'd contracted COVID, but he decided to race anyway.

Now, some people were disappointed with his outcome because he was favored to win both heats and have a glorious story to tell, but I think his story is still glorious. The odds were against him to not be able to compete, let alone place at all, and he tried anyway with the odds stacked against him.

The young man had COVID and asthma and still earned a bronze medal! When asked by a reporter how he felt, he said, "I'm proud of myself!" I, too, was impressed.

Lyles demonstrated exactly the point I'm trying to make to you. Fear of failing can keep you from failing temporarily, but it can also keep you from achieving permanently. You owe it to yourself to do your best. Make an effort. Try anyway in the face of fear.

I recall being afraid of starting a new business. I wanted to start a consulting practice as an additional stream of income, but I couldn't think of a business name. After toying with the idea for what seemed like a lifetime, I had dinner with a friend one night who is a lawyer. He said, "Call it anything. You know you can always change a business name, right?" For whatever reason, that freed me from a 5-year stagnation. I named my business and had my first contract within 3 months!

I was waiting for the perfect name, the perfect prospects, the perfect bank set up and the perfect partnerships. Truth moment: EVERYTHING IN LIFE WILL NOT BE PERFECT! That doesn't mean the world is over. That doesn't mean you won't succeed. Waiting for perfection will have you waiting until you look like that one meme; a skeleton sitting in a chair with her legs crossed and hand on her chin. Stop waiting for perfection and just pick a place and start.

Besides fear, another area we struggle with is "worry". I was speaking with a business colleague on a Friday afternoon. At the end of the conversation, my colleague, Lana asked if I had anything big planned for the weekend. I told her I would be working on my book (not this one, but the next one). She was impressed and asked more about it. I told her it was long overdue as I hadn't published my own book in the last 13 years since I was helping other people with their books. My colleague said she was proud of me. Then, I asked if she had any big plans for the weekend. She told me she was packing up her son to go to Europe for a pilgrimage.

"I just have to work on myself because I get so anxious and worried, you know?"

she said.

"Yes, oh my God," I said, overwhelmed with my next thought, "My book is for you!"

"Really?", she replied, excitedly.
"Yes!"

I told her briefly that I was writing about how to live a life that's light and free to help people release themselves from unnecessary stress and worry. Then, I encouraged her. "You just have to pray and let life happen. Grace can carry you much farther than your will can."

I came across a quote by Dan Zadra, a world-renowned author, where he said, "Worry is a misuse of imagination." When you worry, you are essentially spending time thinking about an issue, overly concerned that the conclusion of the matter will not be in your favor. Might that fallout occur? Sure. But it is also true that it could turn out exactly how you wanted it to or even better.

The worst part of worrying, to me, is the impact on your physical and mental health. Any doctor will tell you that worrying causes stress and stress leads to all types of diseases. Any woman will tell you that, because she worries, she cannot eat, she cannot sleep, nor can she think straight. How do we snap out of it? It's not a snap. It's a decision.

I used to worry about not being able to handle a $400 emergency because statistics at the time said that most Americans could not handle a $400 emergency. What kind of emergency is that? It could be replacing 2 tires, a broken faucet, or a prescription that's not covered by insurance. (All of that has happened to me!) Today, according to a 2024 Bankrate annual emergency savings report, 56% of Americans cannot afford a $1,000 emergency without credit cards or borrowing from friends or family[1].

Instead of worrying about not being able to take care of an emergency, I focused on creating an emergency savings plan. I used one of my accounts to put extra money in for that purpose only. I sought advice from my mother, mentors and financial experts on options to create a budget and make savings a part of my plan. I did

---

[1] https://www.bankrate.com/banking/savings/emergency-savings-report/

not get it right the first month, but with focus and discipline, I eventually saved the $400 and then $1,000. Before long, I was teaching others how to do it. They thought I was just teaching them, but I was also encouraging myself to save even more. Today, if I had to buy a car with cash in an emergency, I could do it without a single worry.

You have to make a decision that you will do one thing each day to reduce stress from your life. No one knows what you worry about more than you. We all have concerns about many areas of our lives, but worry is something that you choose. It may come easy for you to handle money issues, but maybe you worry about your family. I've had that, too. I had many sleepless nights worried about my mother's health. I

Be **F.R.E.E.**

did everything I could to support her when she wasn't well.

I took my mom to doctors' appointments. I spoke with doctors. I picked up prescriptions. At one time (when it was the worst) I slept in her bedroom on the floor to be with her 24 hours a day. Even then, some people thought I wasn't doing enough. They had no idea what I was doing. I prayed, but I still worried. Believe it or not, it wasn't until I stopped worrying that I saw her begin to get better.

So relax. Breathe. Strive for excellence and allow life to happen. Then, put every outcome in God's hands. Where you fail, God will prevail. Please don't misunderstand me. I'm not saying don't plan. I'm not suggesting you don't take the necessary steps to achieve your goals and just throw caution to the wind. Do everything you can to accomplish your goals. Do your best.

Just understand that life happens - meaning there are external factors, out of your control, that will contribute to the outcome whether you like it or not. You cannot control every agent you interact with, every circumstance you are presented with, or every moment in time. You can, however, take the same energy you use to worry to hope for the best.

Questions for Consideration

1. What have you wanted to be perfect that you now realize doesn't need to be perfect?

Be F.R.E.E.

2. What are you ready to try again?
3. What plan can you create to replace your worry?
4. What is something you can do today to relieve stress?
5. What decision do you need to make now to prevent you from worrying later?

Affirmation: I do not have to be perfect. I am human. Humans try things and humans fail. But I can learn from my mistakes and I can try again to succeed. I can replace worry with a plan and a prayer.

EMBRACE YOUR FUTURE

When you think about the future, what comes to mind? I have taken several personality tests over the years and there is one characteristic that is consistent for me. I have a gift for looking ahead and when I see the future, I can put together a path to get to what I see. For me, the future is a blank slate. Dates are predetermined, but where I am and what I'm doing depends on a lot of factors and the primary factor is me. When I think about the future now, I smile. But it hasn't always been that way.

Some years ago, I was overcome with immense sadness. It was just a day, at first. Then, a significant period of time passed - weeks, months even. I couldn't put my finger on why I was so sad. By the time I was 38, I had already been promoted to an executive position, I had built a house and I was driving a brand-new car. I reconnected with my church and found my place in ministry, but something was missing. I still felt lost.

Suddenly, it hit me - I realized I didn't have any more dreams. I had no more big goals. I couldn't picture the next big thing. I couldn't see anything in the future. I am the type of person who needs that guiding light or "North Star", otherwise, my daily routine is an unfulfilling, monotonous schedule of tasks. I felt hopeless. I thought maybe if I started focusing on having a family that would help me get new direction. That didn't work either.

Tiffanie Y. Lewis

After a series of disappointments with things and relationships, I spent time reflecting on feeling joy from the inside out. As I attend several workshops, conferences and meetings, I don't recall where I was or who was speaking at this particular time, but I remember hearing the speaker say, "Smile with your whole body." I closed my eyes and tried to feel a smile with every part of my body. I imagined my toes smiling as I spread them out. I extended my legs and let them smile as I stretched them. I kept going until I smiled with my brain.

As I did this, I could feel my lips curl and part to reveal my pearly whites. I realized that my brain is my favorite part of me. I love the way I think. I love the ideas I'm able to generate. I love that I can come

ℬ F.R.E.E.

up with several ways to solve problems in a short period of time. What's your favorite part of you? What do you absolutely and unequivocally love about yourself? Maybe you've never thought about it before. Well, here's your opportunity! Try the exercise and see what you discover. You need to tap into that discovery in order to see a bright future for yourself.

The future represents opportunities, potential and possibilities. These are all abstract concepts until the outcome is in front of you. The outcomes of the opportunities we take, the potential we have or the possibilities that exist are not known to any of us, initially. Yet, the actions we take each day contribute to those outcomes. Let's talk about each of these related concepts.

Opportunities represent taking chances. When an opportunity to do something is presented, you need decide whether you will accept it, defer it or reject it. On an episode of The Golden Girls, Dorothy said to Rose, "Oh, honey, I know what you're going through. The bottom line is, if you take a chance in life, sometimes good things happen, sometimes bad things happen, but honey, if you don't take a chance, nothing happens." Then, Rose excitedly says, "I'm gonna take a chance!" So be like Rose and take a chance. If the outcome isn't what you desire, remember it's not your last chance. Try something different next time. Just don't give up.

Potential is a tricky thing sometimes. People are always evaluating your potential. They surmise how well you will succeed, how far you will go and how much you can do. However, they are just predicting based on their own perspectives. They do not know all the factors that will contribute to your future results. They are guessing! In fact, they may have data points about you that suggest you have a low probability of achieving a positive result. The thing about probabilities is that it doesn't matter how high or how low they are. There are always unknown factors that can change an outcome. Let's discuss three examples.

One unknown factor is your sheer will and determination. Internal motivation is a serious X-factor that is 100% controlled by you. No one can measure how badly you want something and no one knows what you're willing to do to get it. They don't know that when you want to keep your job while you cultivate a new business venture, you will do it regardless of them saying it's not possible. They don't know that when you want to travel the world and go on at least one international trip per year, you'll do it regardless of who goes with you. They don't know that you want to be in a position to buy a new pair of shoes every time you get paid because you were raised as a middle child and always had hand-me-downs.

No one knows your full story. They only know what they see and what they hear. They don't know what you think or how you feel. Only God knows the real you. And only He knows your limitations. He's the only one that knows exactly how far you can go. Everyone else is just… you know what I'm about to say, right? Guessing!

Another unknown factor is the support of your tribe. Your community can lift you up or let you down. It is up to you to manage your circle. I used to think that blood family members were always going to support you and always be close to you. I learned that the Bible is right - a brother is born in adversity. When you go through something and a person is there with you with unconditional love, he or she becomes closer than a brother.

My dear friend, Valerie, is a tremendous support for me. We can laugh about our misfortunes at work and we can cry when we are overjoyed. She is one friend who I call when I need to vent and when I need to pray. When our mothers were going through something, we were always ready to fly and be with each other – if we weren't already close. She is my sister-friend for life. During your most difficult moments, when you recognize that certain people are not with you (and you thought they would be), perhaps you need to re-evaluate your tribe.

The last unknown factor I want to share with you is about miracles. We know they happen. We don't know how they happen. We do know that unexpected outcomes occur in our favor and all we had was faith. Have you ever been in a situa-

Be F.R.E.E.

tion where what you needed money could not buy, time was running out and space was limited? Have you ever sat, stood or laid down with tears in your eyes, knowing that you had absolutely nothing to offer the situation but hope and prayer? And then, suddenly, it happens. You get a call. You got a letter. You check your account. You stumble upon the very thing that you need through no goodness of your own. It was a miracle!

You don't know how many moving parts in the world had to move like cogs in a wheel to make something happen for you in an inexplicable way. At that moment, you didn't care, did you? Like me, you were probably grateful beyond measure. A miracle is the best unknown factor the world has ever seen and there are more where that came from.

Possibilities are those infinite number of outcomes that can occur when one action leads to another. Often, we are so stuck in the past or our present circumstances that we cannot see that positive outcomes are possible. Life has a way of doing that to us. Its curve balls never stop coming. What has to change is how we handle them.

My grandfather was a profound visionary and an incredibly optimistic thinker. I admired him greatly along with many people for whom his voice echoes all over the world. He was a pastor with the kind of faith that seemed unattainable. When he believed in something with his whole being, he talked about it until you believed it as much as he did. I chuckled because his enthusiasm for things came across as pure passion, even when he didn't fully understand all it entailed.

My grandfather often told the story of how he had to fly to see one of his children who had had a bad accident. He simply said, "I need a jet plane." He couldn't afford a private plane and, quiet as it was kept, he couldn't afford an emergency flight. He went to the airport anyway and told the airline that he needed to get to a certain city. I don't know what he told those people and I don't know how long it took, but he got a seat on a plane to see my uncle.

I recall my grandfather saying repeatedly, "My present position does not determine my future potential in God." He did not waver in his belief that he could get to his destination and he wasn't deterred by what seemed impossible. He knew he needed a plane. He didn't know how he would get one and he didn't care about the "how". He focused on the "what" and the "why". My grandfather did not concern himself with the "how", "when", "where", or who". Sometimes you need to choose one or two of those questions to focus on and let your faith lead you to the rest.

In life, we are presented with opportunities that have potential for great possibilities. It is our responsibility to choose powerfully how to pursue them—one day and one decision at a time. You may be just one decision away from changing the rest of your life.

Questions for Consideration

1. What is your favorite part of you?
2. What about the future makes you smile?
3. What are you willing to take a chance on?
4. What kind of person might you need to add to your tribe?
5. What do you need to focus on and where do you need to allow your faith to kick in?

Affirmation: I will embrace the future with a smile. I will take a chance to pursue my dreams in the face of adversity. I will be free to always be me.

Be

F*orget the past*

R*emember who you are*

E*merge from failures and worry*

E*mbrace your future*

NOTES

www.ingramcontent.com/pod-product-compliance
Lightning Source LLC
Chambersburg PA
CBHW060538030426
42337CB00021B/4318